# *Carnation, Lily, Lily, Rose*

## The Story of a Painting

By HUGH BREWSTER
with paintings by
JOHN SINGER SARGENT

The summer I was five,
John Singer Sargent came to visit us.
He wasn't a famous artist then.
But he painted a picture in our garden
that became quite famous.
Here is how I remember what happened ...

KIDS CAN PRESS

THE GREEN BROADWAY WORCS.

We lived at Farnham House, beside the village green in Broadway. My parents, Frank and Lily Millet, were Americans, but they loved living in an old English village. Soon many of my father's artist friends came to visit us there.

## Part I: August 1885

I woke up because I heard my name.

Downstairs the grown-ups were talking and laughing. I couldn't make out what they were saying, but you can always hear your own name.

Then I heard it again. I think it was Papa's voice, saying "Kate."

Why were they talking about me?

I slipped out of bed and went to the top of the stairs.

The parlor door was open, and I could smell smoke from my father's pipe. I could hear Ned Abbey telling a story. Ned and his friend John Sargent had arrived at our house that afternoon from a boating trip on the River Thames. We all loved Ned — he was always so full of laughter and jokes. But I felt shy around his friend, Mr. Sargent. When Ned introduced me to him, he only nodded his bristling, black beard at me. And he had a big, white bandage wrapped around his head that made him look fierce — like a pirate.

As I slowly crept down the stairs, Aunt Lucia suddenly appeared in the hallway. "Look who's here!" she said as she scooped me up and carried me into the parlor.

"Well, Kate, my sleepyhead," said Mama as we sat down by the fireplace. "Mr. Sargent wants *you* to be in his painting!"

At breakfast the next day, Ned Abbey told me why Mr. Sargent was wearing such a big bandage. On their boating trip he had dived into the river and struck a spike in a log under the water. When he came to the surface, blood was pouring from a gash in his head. This accident was the reason they had come to visit us in Broadway a little sooner than planned. While Mr. Sargent's wound healed, they would take country walks and sketch and paint.

Mr. Sargent was very excited about something they had seen from their boat on the river. One evening at twilight they had watched some children lighting paper lanterns hung between rose bushes in a garden. Ned said it was a magical scene and that Mr. Sargent had drawn a quick sketch of it.

"John is determined to make it into a painting that will make people simply *rave* with pleasure," said Ned.

"And you'll make such a good little model for it, won't you, Kate?"

"Yes," I replied, but inside I wasn't so sure. I had seen models posing while my father painted them. They had to stand very still for hours and hours! And I wasn't certain that Mr. Sargent liked me very much. But Ned said he was just shy.

*A few years after his boating trip with Ned Abbey, Mr. Sargent painted a picture of another boating party on the River Avon, not far from Broadway.*

Mr. Sargent started painting outdoors that same day. From an upstairs window I watched him as he carried his easel into the fields beyond our garden. When he saw something he liked, he would suddenly stop, plant his easel and start painting. This certainly wasn't the way my father and Ned Abbey painted. They liked to work indoors with models and costumes, recreating scenes from history.

Papa explained to us at teatime that painting in the open air was the latest style in France. He said that these French painters, called Impressionists, tried to capture the light and color they saw in nature. "Sometimes with just little blobs or dribbles," he said with a wry smile. There was much talk about a man named Monet. Ned whispered to me that Mr. Sargent had recently visited this famous painter Monet and painted a picture of him painting outdoors.

While visiting Claude Monet at his home in Giverny, France, Mr. Sargent painted him working at his easel by the edge of a wood. After this visit Mr. Sargent was inspired to do more painting in the open air.

8

One afternoon I was playing in the garden with my friend Tessa Gosse, when Mr. Sargent suddenly appeared. He called out to us,

"Stay just as you are!
    And don't move.
I must make a sketch of you."

We both froze like statues while Mr. Sargent circled around and made quick drawings in his sketchbook. When he was done, he just nodded to us and left.

Tessa (whose father was a writer) shrugged and said knowingly,

"Oh, artists!"

For her eighth
birthday party on
September 14, 1885,
Tessa Gosse
wore a white dress
and put autumn flowers
called colchicums
in her hair. Mr. Sargent
admired the purple
blooms set against
Tessa's red hair
and painted this color
sketch of her
on the spot.

Everyone seemed to be involved in the plans for Mr. Sargent's "big picture." Aunt Lucia was sewing a white smock for me to wear. Mama had ordered Chinese paper lanterns from Cheltenham for me to light.

*And I had to be a blonde!*

Mr. Sargent thought my hair was too dark, so Ned Abbey had found a yellow wig for me to wear.

Late one afternoon the paper lanterns were strung between two rose bushes in the garden, and tall, white lilies in pots were placed nearby. When all was ready, Mr. Sargent appeared with his sketchbook and a white hat on his head instead of the bandage.

He quietly stood me next to a lantern with my head slightly bent. Then he began sketching. It was hard to stand still. The wig felt hot and itchy. I didn't like everyone watching me. And Mr. Sargent seemed a little annoyed whenever I moved or looked up. He tried me in several poses and scribbled away in his sketchbook.

After a while he closed it, nodded and said, "Thank you, Kate," and gave me a wrapped candy.

Aunt Lucia came and hugged me, and Mama and Papa clapped. Then we all went inside for tea. Everyone said I'd done very well, and Aunt Lucia gave me a second slice of cake. But I couldn't really tell if Mr. Sargent was pleased with me or not.

Mr. Sargent
loved to
sketch and
paint lilies.
He used tall
lilies in pots
for this
picture of
Billy and Edith
Vickers that
he painted in
1884, a year
before he
came to
Broadway.

I soon got used to posing for Mr. Sargent every day in the garden. But it was hard to stand very, very still. One day two men carried an absolutely HUGE white canvas out of the barn. It was far too big to put on an easel, so it sat on the ground held up by some pieces of wood. Mr. Sargent had to peer around the side of it to see me. He would look fiercely at me and then make wide strokes over the canvas with a piece of charcoal. I tried holding my breath so as not to move

That was the same day the Barnards came to visit. I remember Mr. Frederick Barnard (another artist!) coming through the gate in his straw hat. He was followed by his wife and two daughters, Polly, aged eleven, and Dorothy (nicknamed Dolly), who was seven. I saw that Polly and Dolly both had fair hair and beautiful curls. Mr. Sargent saw it, too.

Things then happened very fast. Within minutes I was standing off to one side and Polly and Dolly were holding the lanterns between the rose bushes. Mr. Sargent circled around, placing them in different poses. Then he walked over to my parents and the Barnards, puffing a little under his beard.

"Well, er—um, that is, I think— we should have two children in the picture— yes, two children."

Aunt Lucia came over, kneeled next to me and took off my yellow wig. She whispered that Mr. Sargent wanted to paint Polly and Dolly instead of me. She said it was because they were taller and had lighter hair. But Mr. Sargent would paint a portrait of just me, later, she said.

I didn't come downstairs for supper that night.

I stayed in my room, and I cried.

From these sketches Mr. Sargent
made of Dolly (left) and Polly (right), it's easy
to see why he wanted them in his painting.
He also made several drawings of
Chinese lanterns in his sketchbook, trying them
out in different positions.

13

"I hate Polly, and I hate Dolly.
Now they're here I'm not very jolly…"

I sang this little song to myself as I kept to my room over the next two days.
I hated Mr. Sargent, too, and wished that he'd never come to Broadway. Aunt Lucia
noticed my glum mood and tried to cheer me up. But she was very busy helping
Mrs. Barnard make smocks for Polly and Dolly to wear for Mr. Sargent's painting.
Mama was busy with my baby brother, who had a chest cold. And Tessa was spending
most of her time with her new best friends, Polly and Dolly. One afternoon, when
I looked out my bedroom window, I saw them walking together on the village green.

Not long after that I heard music and looked out
the window again. A small band was playing on
the green. There was a trumpet player, some
tubas and a trombone and a man thumping on
a big bass drum. Soon I heard the knocker at
our front door, and then Polly Barnard was
standing at my bedroom door. She said
breathlessly,

"Our mother has
hired the band. We're
all having a parade!
You must come!"

Mr. Sargent drew a quick sketch of the band in a letter to his sister (opposite). I could easily hear the music through my window (right) since my room at Farnham House (above) looked down on the village green. My window can be seen above the horse-drawn cart.

Mr. Sargent's painting, *Village Children*, was painted a few years after
he visited us in Broadway. Little girls were expected to wear hats in those days.
For our parade around the green, many of us wore flowers or leaves in our hair
instead, while Dolly Barnard and I waved flags.

I followed Polly downstairs and out onto the green. Mrs. Barnard was handing out flowers and branches with colored leaves to the children. She put a wreath of red roses on my head.

"Kate will lead the parade," Mrs. Barnard called out over the noise and asked the children to line up behind me. She gave me an American flag to carry, and the band struck up a lively tune. As we marched around the green, I saw that Dolly was waving the Union Jack and that the others were bedecked in flowers and leaves.

The Lygon Arms

When we arrived at our house, Aunt Lucia opened the front door, and we all trooped through to the garden. There I sang "Yankee Doodle" and the others sang "Rule Britannia," and we waved our flags and branches as the adults clapped. Then we sang "Happy Birthday" to Mama. (I'd forgotten it was her birthday!)

That night all the grown-ups went to the town's inn, the Lygon Arms, for Mama's birthday dinner. Afterward my mother and Mr. Sargent sang duets. Aunt Lucia told me that Mr. Sargent wasn't so shy when he sat down at the piano. He could play dozens of tunes by heart and would sing along with great gusto.

I felt much better after the parade. And Tessa and Polly and Dolly were all being very nice to me. I didn't want to be in the garden at teatime, however, when everyone gathered to watch Mr. Sargent paint his "big picture." But Aunt Lucia said,

"I can't possibly manage it all, Kate,
if you don't help me."

So on that afternoon, and others that followed, I held the string as we hung the paper lanterns between the rose bushes. Then Aunt Lucia would place the pots of white lilies nearby. After that, Mr. Sargent would find someone to help him bring his big white canvas out of the barn and prop it up on the lawn. Polly and Dolly would then appear in their white smocks. Then we would all wait ... and wait ... and wait ... while the adults played lawn tennis.

In a letter to his sister (above), Mr. Sargent drew a sketch of his "big" painting, showing lanterns strung between the rose bushes. He describes it as a "fearful difficult subject." In a cartoon (opposite) he makes fun of his painting style at the sessions that followed afternoon tennis. Other caricatures show Mr. Gosse (center) and Ned Abbey (bottom) on the tennis court.

Just as the sun started to go down behind the trees, the tennis players would suddenly throw down their rackets and charge toward us. The lanterns would be lit. Mr. Sargent would stand at a little distance from the easel and then run forward to rapidly dab paint on the picture. His brush would twitch like a bird's tail. He would look at Polly and Dolly and the glowing lanterns and then dab at the painting again.

This went on for ten or maybe twenty minutes each evening when the light was just right. Papa explained that Mr. Sargent was trying to capture that special time at twilight when colors like pinks and reds stand out as the lamps begin to glow. But he said it was an awfully difficult thing to do.

Mr. Sargent never seemed satisfied. Every morning Tessa and I would look in the barn and see the big canvas with all the paint scraped right off it. "Poor Polly and Dolly," said Tessa. "This painting will *never* be done!"

On our river trip we saw people asleep by the shore in flat-bottomed boats called punts. Mr. Sargent must have liked what he saw since he did several paintings like this one. A postcard (opposite) shows steam launches by the bridge at Evesham, where we started our boat trip.

Mr. Sargent continued to paint Polly and Dolly each evening right through September, if it wasn't raining. When the flowers in our garden faded, Mr. Sargent walked around the village and offered to buy flowers from other people's gardens! Tessa said that the villagers all thought "them Americans" (as they called us) were raving mad, anyhow. She and the Barnard girls loved to make fun of my Massachusetts accent. But Ned Abbey said he thought that the English were *much* odder than we were. And he made fun of *their* accents!

One day Ned took us all on a boat trip on the Avon River in a steam launch hired by his friend, the painter Alfred Parsons. We had a huge English picnic lunch with a roast goose, ham, tongue, rabbit pie and pickled walnuts. The whole deck of the boat was covered with plates!

Mr. Sargent came along with his friend Henry James. They sat in the bow of the boat and talked very seriously. Tessa said her father told her that Mr. James was a famous author and "quite a good one — for an American," she added with a poke to my ribs. I decided to sit next to Ned in the stern while he played his banjo and sang American songs like "Swanee River" — but with his own words.

"Way down upon the Avon River,
      far, far away,
That's where
      our boat is
churning ever,
   That's where the
art folks play."

By November there was snow on the hills in the mornings, and most of the summer visitors had left. But Polly and Dolly still had to stand by the rose bushes every afternoon while Mr. Sargent painted. They wore woolen cardigans under their smocks, and Mr. Sargent was wrapped up like an Arctic explorer. The rose bushes were brown and bare, so Aunt Lucia tied some artificial flowers from one of Mama's old hats onto the branches.

I watched from the window as Polly and Dolly shivered outside. I was glad it was them and not me.

Soon even Mr. Sargent realized it was too cold to finish the painting, so it was taken off its frame, rolled up and stored in the barn. Aunt Lucia said Mr. Sargent was going down to Bournemouth to paint a portrait of Robert Louis Stevenson. He was the author of *Treasure Island* — a book that Papa had been reading to me at bedtime!

But Mr. Sargent came back for Christmas and brought wonderful presents. He gave Aunt Lucia a beautiful Japanese screen. For me he had the most marvelous dollhouse with painted rooms and tiny lights that glowed through the windows. "It reminded me of happy evenings in Broadway with the Millets," he said.

I loved it! And I was even beginning to like Mr. Sargent.

22

(Opposite) Mr. Sargent is dressed warmly as he works on his large canvas propped up beside the barn. (Above) In November he also painted the fields behind Farnham House. He even included the shadow of him working at his easel in the painting.

## PART II: JULY 1886

The next summer even more people came to Broadway.
And we had moved to a bigger old stone house called Russell
House. It had rooms for more visitors as well as a huge garden
with a lily pond, two gazebos and an orchard. Aunt Lucia had
supervised all the painting and decorating at Russell House
while my parents had been in America during the winter. In
April Mr. Sargent had sent fifty lily bulbs to Aunt Lucia. Twenty
were to be put into pots for his "big picture," and the rest were
for the garden.

Another gift from Mr. Sargent for the garden was
a large blue peacock! Tessa Gosse's parents had given it to
him, and he liked to sketch it.

*But it had a horrible loud screech
and used to chase me and bite
me on the legs.*

I wasn't at all
sorry when it
was found lying
dead one
morning by the
garden wall.

Russell House was around the corner from Farnham House, at the edge of the village.
The stone barn attached to it was made into a studio by Ned Abbey.
Mr. Sargent made many sketches of the peacock (left) as it strutted around the garden.

In this picture of our garden, the potted lilies stand ready for the afternoon painting sessions

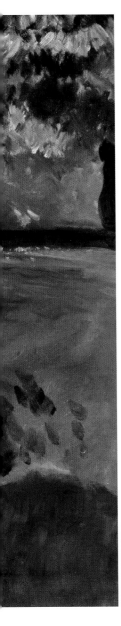

Mr. Sargent was in Europe for part of the summer, but when he returned, his "big picture" was taken out of storage.

"When will you begin painting again?" I asked him.

"My young models are still in London, Kate," he replied. "Their father, it seems, has sprained his ankle."

Tessa and I wondered if we would be asked to pose instead. But then the Barnards arrived, and so the painting sessions began once again.

Around four o'clock each afternoon, Aunt Lucia would pour tea and pass out cakes from a table in the garden. I would dash about with the other children while Polly and Dolly waited by the rose bushes. We would hear shouts from the tennis game and then suddenly

Mr. Sargent would run over, pick up his brush and begin painting for as long as the light lasted.

By the end of summer, the painting was no longer being scraped down. And Mr. Sargent had shortened the width of the canvas to make it more square. When I peeked at it in the barn, I could see two girls' heads and the orange glowing circles of the lanterns.

A cartoon shows Mr. Sargent at work while the tennis game continues behind him.

Mr. Sargent's portrait of Mama captures just how beautiful she was. His sketch of Ned Abbey (below), however, doesn't show his big, friendly grin. Even this broken chair caught Mr. Sargent's eye.

During the mornings Mr. Sargent would once again tramp off with his easel and paint outdoors. He painted Russell House from the orchard, harvesters resting in the nearby fields — and even an old broken chair in our garden.

And it seemed like *everyone* was posing for a portrait by Mr. Sargent. Tessa Gosse and her father and Mrs. Barnard had all been painted by him. Now he was painting Mama in a white dress with a blue shawl and had even begun sketching my baby brother Laurence. But what about me? Aunt Lucia had promised that he would paint a picture of just me!

Ned Abbey had a studio in the stone barn next to Russell House. I liked to visit there as he had lots of costumes (for his historical paintings) that he would let me dress up in. One day I asked him why everyone was being painted by Mr. Sargent except me. Ned smiled a big smile that showed his gold tooth. He picked me up and swung me about, saying,

"Oh, Kate, it's not fair that your hair's not fair, but you're my fair maid and my fairy queen!"

In the evenings Ned's studio was where the grown-ups gathered for music and card games and dancing. Aunt Lucia would tell me about the parties at breakfast. One night she waltzed seven times with Henry James, and everyone teased her and said she might show up as a character in one of his novels!

But by early September plans were afoot for the biggest party of all.

This was for Mama's birthday on the eighteenth. Aunt Lucia decided to have a long table decorated with flowers set up in the studio. I carried the baskets while she cut masses of flowers from the garden. And Mr. Sargent, Mr. Barnard and another artist were drawing funny cartoons of each of the guests for the place cards.

Mr. Sargent sketched Mama helping me with my shoe. Later he painted me helping Aunt Lucia gather rose petals. The painting is called a "study" because it's not finished. I wish he had at least drawn in my face!

31

Then Tessa's uncle, Mr. Alma Tadema, came up with another idea. (Tessa said he was a *very* famous artist who had met the queen.) Mr. Alma Tadema decided that everyone would wear wreaths made of flowers on their heads — just like in an ancient Roman festival.

My father said the men would never do it, but he ended up with a wreath of red double dahlias on his head! And Mr. Gosse wore pink roses! Aunt Lucia was crowned with yellow dahlias while Mama looked absolutely beautiful in a new white dress and a wreath of red tea roses. And I was allowed to stay up for the entertainment!

Place cards show the cartoons for Mama (top), Aunt Lucia (middle) and Mr. Comyns-Carr (bottom), a witty Irishman who wrote verses on the back of each card.

Mr. Alma Tadema
insisted that everyone
wear flower wreaths
for Mama's party —
just like in his painting
of a Roman spring
festival.

(Above) This page from one of Mr. Sargent's sketchbooks reminds me of the musical evening at Mama's birthday party. (Right) The sheet music for "The Wreath," which was also called "Ye Shepherds Tell Me." It had a repeating chorus with the words "Carnation, lily, lily, rose."

I was sitting in Aunt Lucia's lap when Mr. Sargent sat down at the piano after dinner. Mr. Gosse and Mr. Parsons joined him in singing a trio called "The Wreath." It was a flowery, old song about shepherds and shepherdesses. Mr. Sargent sang the first verse in his booming voice:

*Ye shepherds tell me have you seen*
*My Flora pass this way*
*In shape and feature, beauty's queen,*
*In pastoral array*

Mr. Parsons sang the second verse:

*A wreath around her head she wore*
*Carnation, lily, lily, rose*
*And in her hand a crook she bore*
*And sweets her breath compose.*

Mr. Gosse

Since Mama's name was Lily, he bowed to her each time he sang the word "lily." Mr. Gosse did the same when he sang the third verse, which was about "hands lily white and cheeks of rosy hue." Between each verse there was a rousing chorus that the three men sang together in perfect harmony.

Aunt Lucia and I cheered and clapped at the end along with everyone else. To cries of "Encore!" the men sang it at least three more times.

For days afterward I heard people humming the "Carnation, lily" chorus.

I think Polly and Dolly and Tessa were jealous that I had been there and they hadn't.

As the days grew colder in September, the summer visitors began to leave. Every day we could see that Mr. Sargent's "big picture" was becoming more and more finished. I could even recognize Polly and Dolly's faces on the canvas.

Mama was still posing for her portrait. One morning when Mama had a bad cold, Mr. Sargent turned to me and said, "All right, Kate, today it's your turn." I wanted to show him that I was much older than last year, so when he sketched me, I looked right at him and tried hard not to wriggle.

Mr. Sargent made color studies of Polly (left) and Dolly (above) to help him choose the right poses for the painting.

Aunt Lucia was sending a letter that day to my grandparents in Massachusetts and asked me to add a message for them. Across the bottom of the letter I printed,

*"I am having my portrait painted in the studio."*

By October the Barnards and the Gosses were ready to go back to London. Mr. Sargent, too, was preparing to leave. He could now finish his big picture in his studio in London.

To celebrate the last afternoon, we went to a large field

Aunt Lucia's letters home described all the activity at Russell House. She wrote about Mr. Sargent painting this portrait of me.

and flew Japanese kites. Even Mr. Sargent came along for the fun. When we went back to the house, there was a package in brown paper sitting on the mantelpiece. It had "Kate" printed on it. Mr. Sargent picked me up and took me over to it. I tore off the paper and saw myself staring back.

*It was my portrait—and it looked just like me!*

Everyone clapped, and I gave Mr Sargent a kiss on his rough, bearded cheek. He turned very red but patted my head kindly.

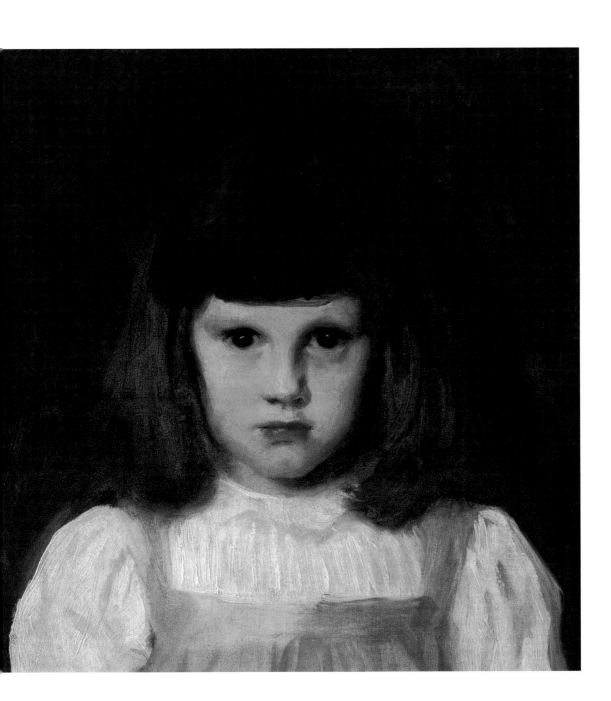

# Part III: June 1887

The gallery walls at the Royal Academy were crowded with paintings. But Mr. Sargent's *Carnation, Lily, Lily, Rose* (opposite) drew the most attention.

We went home to America that winter, but by June we were back at Russell House in Broadway. I remember taking the train down to London with Mama and Papa. And I remember taking Papa's arm as we walked into a huge gallery that was lined with all kinds of paintings.

All of a sudden we saw Mr. Sargent's "big picture." Even among all the other paintings it still stood out. We walked straight to it and formed a little crowd in front of it. The paper lanterns and the flowers looked just as they had at twilight in our garden. And the picture *glowed*! It seemed like the light was actually coming from *inside* the canvas.

"By golly, he's done it," said Papa.

"*Carnation, Lily, Lily, Rose*," said one man, reading the title in his catalog. "I wonder what he means by calling it that."

But I knew what it meant! I tugged at Papa's sleeve.

"Papa, Papa, it's from the song! He's named the picture for the song! The song for Mama's birthday!"

# Epilogue

*Carnation, Lily, Lily, Rose* was the most talked-about painting in London that season. The Royal Academy decided to purchase it as a gift to the nation — a real honor for an artist who wasn't British.

The Millet family stayed at Russell House in Broadway for many years, although Kate's father continued to travel the world for his painting and writing. In April of 1912, he was going to New York on board the RMS *Titanic* when it struck an iceberg. He was last seen helping women and children into lifeboats. By then Kate was married and had children of her own and was living in Winchcombe, a town not far from Broadway.

Today *Carnation, Lily, Lily, Rose* hangs in the Tate Gallery in London and thousands of people come to see it every year. The lanterns still glow just as they did in that summer garden in Broadway over a hundred years ago.

(Opposite, left) Kate poses at age twelve in a Japanese costume possibly brought back by her father from one of his trips to the Far East. As a young woman (opposite, top) she was photographed in a stylish gown before a ball. In 1906 she married Frank Adlard (center), and together they raised six children and lived into their seventies (bottom).

# BIOGRAPHIES

**John Singer Sargent** (1856–1925) spent two summers in Broadway that not only produced one of his greatest paintings — they also changed his life.

When he first arrived there in August of 1885, he was feeling quite discouraged about his career as an artist. He even talked with Edmund Gosse (Tessa's father) about giving up painting altogether. When Mr. Gosse asked him what he would do instead, Sargent replied that he might become a businessman or "go in for music, don't you know."

*Sargent stands in his Paris studio beside* Madame X, *a portrait that is now hailed as one of his masterpieces.*

Just over a year before, John Sargent had been considered one of the most promising young artists in Paris. His paintings had been praised when they were exhibited each year at the Salon, the most important art show in Paris. For the Salon of 1884, he had worked very hard on a portrait of a beautiful society lady in an elegant black dress. But the painting caused a huge fuss — many people thought it was both shocking and ugly! Later called *Madame X,* this portrait left Sargent's reputation in tatters. Broadway proved to be just the right place to restore his spirits. Sargent loved the fresh air and beautiful countryside and thrived on the companionship of the other artists. He also liked the warm family life he found at Farnham House — perhaps because as a boy he had never really had a proper home.

John Sargent had been born in 1856 in Florence, Italy, to American parents. The family lived in hotels and lodgings as they moved from place to place in Europe.

Sargent grew up speaking several languages and acquired a great passion for art and architecture. His talent for sketching and painting was encouraged by his mother, who liked to paint watercolors. In 1874, he went to Paris to study painting. A few years later, he began receiving commissions to paint portraits of prominent Parisians. After the scandal of *Madame X*, however, the commissions stopped. By 1886, Sargent had packed up his Paris studio and moved to London. But it would be in America that his career would take flight.

In 1890, Sargent spent ten months painting portraits in the United States. In Boston, he was commissioned to paint murals for the new Boston Public Library — a huge project that he would work on for the next 25 years. By the mid-1890s, Sargent was the most sought-after portrait painter in the world. He often worked from dawn till dusk seven days a week. By 1907, he had had enough and decided to give up portrait painting and do more watercolors, particularly on summer trips he would take to Switzerland and Italy. Often in the Swiss Alps he would be joined by Polly and Dolly Barnard, who sometimes appear in his paintings. The Barnard sisters were also with Sargent at a special dinner held for him on April 14, 1925, after the last murals for the Boston Public Library had been sent off. Later that night he suffered a heart attack while sleeping and was found dead the next morning.

John Singer Sargent left behind a legacy of over 900 oil paintings and more than 2000 watercolors along with thousands of drawings. He had painted everyone from two U.S. presidents to gypsies and street children, and captured scenes that ranged from the canals of Venice to the battlefields of World War I. It seems fitting that Polly and Dolly Barnard were with him on the night he died. As little girls in white smocks forty years before, they had been part of a painting that helped restore Sargent's faith in himself — a painting that would become one of the best-loved works of a great artist.

**Edwin Austen "Ned" Abbey** (1852–1911) was described by Sargent as "a delightful, original genius." Born in Philadelphia, he worked as a magazine illustrator in New York until he went to England at the age of 26, and stayed for the rest of his life. He is known for his carefully researched illustrations for the works of Oliver Goldsmith and Shakespeare and the murals he created for the Boston Public Library, which today stand near those done by his friend John Sargent.

**Alfred Parsons** (1847–1920) was an English landscape painter who became part of the Broadway group through his friendship with Ned Abbey. They had been roommates in London, and they later shared studio space and worked together on illustrations for several books.

**Francis Davis Millet** (1846–1912) painted historical scenes and also murals for a number of U.S. public buildings. But he was a highly energetic man with a broad array of talents and was also a journalist, war correspondent and wrote and translated books. His wife, **Elizabeth "Lily" Millet** (1855–1932), lived on at Russell House after his death on the *Titanic* and became grandmother to the six children of her daughter, **Kate Millet Adlard** (1880–1958), who lived in nearby Winchcombe. **Lucia Millet** (1851–1917), Francis's sister, returned to East Bridgewater, Massachusetts, in late 1886, where

she married and taught in the local school.

**Marion Alice "Polly" Barnard** (1874–1946) and her sister, **Dorothy "Dolly" Barnard** (1878–1949), were the daughters of **Frederick Barnard** (1846–1896), an English artist and illustrator, and **Alice Faraday** (1847–1918). The two sisters never married, remained close friends of Sargent's and were remembered in his will.

**Emily Teresa "Tessa" Gosse** (1877–1951) was the daughter of **Edmund Gosse** (1849–1928), a distinguished literary critic, poet and writer who was knighted in 1925. Tessa attended Cambridge and became a devoted suffragette who campaigned for women to be allowed to vote.

**Henry James** (1843–1916) was a mentor and friend of Sargent's and encouraged him to move to London from Paris in 1886. A famed American novelist (*Daisy Miller, Washington Square, The Turn of the Screw*), he lived in England and wrote about the kind of people Sargent depicts in his portraits.

*Sargent painted this portrait of Dolly Barnard three years after* Carnation, Lily, Lily, Rose.

**Lawrence Alma Tadema** (1836–1912) was a Dutch-born painter of scenes set in ancient times. He moved to England in 1870 and married artist Laura Epps, a sister of Mrs. Gosse. His paintings were popular with the public, and Queen Victoria knighted him in 1899, but after his death his work was dismissed as depictions of "Victorians in togas."

# Paintings and Sketches

P. 31 *Woman and Child*, 1885–86, pencil, Metropolitan Museum of Art, Gift of Mrs. Francis Ormond, 1950, (50.130.119r).

P. 32 (see p. 19).

P. 33 (Right) *Spring* by Lawrence Alma Tadema (detail), 1895, oil on canvas, 70¼ x 31½" (178.4 x 80 cm), J. Paul Getty Museum, Los Angeles, (72.PA.3). (Left) *Self Portrait* by Lawrence Alma Tadema, 1897, © Galleria degli Uffizi, Florence, Italy / The Bridgeman Art Library.

P. 34 *Parlor Concert*, c. 1880s, pencil, Metropolitan Museum of Art, gift of Mrs. Francis Ormond, 1950, (50.130.140i).

P. 35 *Edmund Gosse,* 1886, oil on canvas, 21½ x 17½" (54.6 x 44.5 cm), National Portrait Gallery, London.

P. 36 *Study of Polly Barnard for 'Carnation, Lily, Lily, Rose,'* c. 1885, oil on canvas, 19½ x 15½" (49.5 x 39.3 cm), private collection, photograph courtesy of the Adelson Galleries, New York.

P. 37 *Study of Dorothy Barnard for 'Carnation, Lily, Lily, Rose,'* c. 1885, oil on canvas, 28½ x 18½" (72.3 x 49.5cm), private collection, photograph courtesy of the Adelson Galleries, New York.

P. 39 *Kate Millet,* 1886, oil on canvas, 16 x 14" (40.6 x 35.6 cm), private collection, photograph courtesy of the Adelson Galleries, New York.

P. 41 *Carnation, Lily, Lily, Rose*, 1885–86, oil on canvas, 68½ x 60½" (174 x 153.7 cm), © Tate London, 2006.

P. 45 *Portrait of Dorothy Barnard*, 1889, oil on canvas, 27¼ x 25½" (70.5 x 39.4 cm), © Fitzwilliam Museum, University of Cambridge, UK / The Bridgeman Art Library.

# Selected Bibliography

Adelson, Warren, Stanley Olson and Richard Ormond. *Sargent at Broadway*. New York: Universe, 1986.

Charteris, Evan. *John Sargent.* New York: Charles Scribner's & Sons, 1927.

Gallati, Barbara Dayer. *Great Expectations: John Singer Sargent Painting Children.* New York: Bulfinch, 2004.

Houghton, Colin and Nick Darien Jones. *Broadway Pictorial.* Stroud, U.K: Darien Jones Publishing, 2004.

Kilmurray, Elaine and Richard Ormond. *Sargent.* London: Tate Gallery Publishing, 1998.

Lippincott, Louise. *Lawrence Alma Tadema, 'Spring.'* Malibu: J. Paul Getty Museum, 1991.

Ormond, Richard and Elaine Kilmurray. *John Singer Sargent: The Early Portraits.* New Haven: Yale University Press, 1998.

Olson, Stanley. *John Singer Sargent: His Portrait.* New York: St. Martin's Press, 1986.

Simpson, Marc Alfred. *Reconstructing the Golden Age: American Artists in Broadway, Worcestershire, 1885–1889.* Yale University Dissertation, 1993.

Sharpey-Schafer, Joyce. *Soldier of Fortune, F.D. Millet 1846–1912.* Utica, New York, 1984.

# Photographs / Artifacts

*Every effort has been made to clear copyright and correctly attribute all images. If any errors have occurred, they will be corrected in future editions. Any images not identified here are from private collections.*

Adlard Family Collection: p. 2 (bottom) and all photos on p. 43; Dr. Colin Houghton and Nick Darien Jones from *Broadway Pictorial*: p. 2 (top), p. 14 (top), p. 17, p. 24–25; Bridgeman Art Library: p. 7, photo © The Illustrated London News Picture Library, London, UK; Ian Brewster: p. 15 (bottom); Almonry Heritage Centre, Evesham: p. 21; Fogg Art Museum, Harvard: p. 27, *Photograph of Sargent painting 'Carnation, Lily, Lily, Rose,'* gift of Mrs. Francis Ormond, 1937.7.27.1.A; British Library: p. 27, cover of *Treasure Island*, 1899, 21477/012624.f.3; National Library of Australia: p. 34, *'Ye Shepherds Tell Me'* [music], nla.mus-an 10131401; Archives of American Art, Smithsonian Institution: p. 38, envelope from Francis Davis Millet and Millet Family Papers (1858–1984), and p. 44, photo from Photographs of Artists in their Paris Studios; Mary Evans Picture Library: p. 40, *Royal Academy Visitors*, 1880, 10187687.

Text © 2007 Hugh Brewster
Design and compilation © 2007 Whitfield Editions

Kids Can Press acknowledges the financial support of the Government
of Ontario, through the Ontario Media Development Corporation's
Ontario Book Initiative; the Ontario Arts Council; the Canada Council
for the Arts; and the Government of Canada, through the BPIDP,
for our publishing activity.

Published in Canada by
Kids Can Press Ltd.
29 Birch Avenue
Toronto, ON  M4V 1E2

Published in the U.S. by
Kids Can Press Ltd.
2250 Military Road
Tonawanda, NY  14150

www.kidscanpress.com

The text is set in Perpetua.

Edited by Karen Li
Designed by Gordon Sibley
Produced by Whitfield Editions
Printed and bound in Singapore

This book is smyth sewn casebound.

CM 07   0 9 8 7 6 5 4 3 2 1

**Library and Archives Canada Cataloguing in Publication**

Brewster, Hugh
Carnation, lily, lily, rose : the story of a painting / text by Hugh Brewster ;
with paintings by John Singer Sargent.

ISBN-13: 978-1-55453-137-0
ISBN-10: 1-55453-137-3

1. Sargent, John Singer, 1856–1925.
Carnation, lily, lily, rose—Juvenile fiction.
2. Sargent, John Singer, 1856–1925—Juvenile fiction.
3. Millet, Kate, fl. 1885–1886—Juvenile fiction.
4. Broadway (Worcestershire, England)—Juvenile fiction.
5. Sargent, John Singer, 1856–1925—Juvenile literature.
I. Sargent, John Singer, 1856–1925  II. Title.

PS8603.R49C37 2007       jC813'.6       C2006-906360-5

Kids Can Press is a *corus*™ Entertainment company

# AUTHOR'S NOTE

This is a fictionalized account of the creation of Sargent's famous painting, but it is based on real events. Scenes such as Lily Millet's birthday tribute are imagined. We know that "The Wreath" was a popular tune with the Broadway circle, but we can't be certain that it was sung that evening, though I like to think it was. For the most part, the narrative hews fairly closely to occurrences described in Lucia Millet's letters home and in the recollections of other members of the Broadway circle. The village of Broadway in Worcestershire is very real and remains today much as Kate and Mr. Sargent would remember it.

# ACKNOWLEDGMENTS

The images in this book have come from a wide variety of sources and I'm grateful to all the collectors, museums and archives who have allowed them to be reproduced. Special thanks to: Elizabeth Oustinoff of the John Singer Sargent Catalogue Raisonné at the Adelson Galleries for all her help with sourcing images, and also her colleague, Jay Cantor; Wendy Hurlock-Baker at the Archives of American Art for her cheerful help; Dr. Colin Houghton and Nick Darien Jones for providing archival photos from their book *Broadway Pictorial*. Thanks to: Robert, Edward and Sue Adlard for information and family pictures; John Thorneywork, Elaine Allen-Jone and Michael Houghton for receiving me in Broadway; Michael Rowe of the Almonry Heritage Centre, Evesham; art historians Alison Syme and Peter Engstrom for reviewing the text; Nan Froman and Karen Li for editing: Ian Brewster for photography; Gord Sibley for design; Marc Simpson for his invaluable thesis. Thanks also to Giles Bazeley, Thelma Z. Lenkin, Lee Jacobson, Brian Bixley, Phillipp Andres, Marian Fowler, Valerie Hussey, Paola Cohen, Laurie McGaw and Natasha Wallace of the invaluable JSS Gallery website.